Winter Air Quality in Yellowstone National Park
2006 - 2007

Natural Resource Technical Report NPS/NRPC/ARD/NRTR--2007/065

Dr. John D. Ray
National Park Service
Air Resources Division
Denver, CO 80225
John_D_Ray@nps.gov

November 2007

U.S. Department of the Interior
National Park Service
Natural Resource Program Center
Fort Collins, CO 80525

The Natural Resource Publication series addresses natural resource topics that are of interest and applicability to a broad readership in the National Park Service and to others in the management of natural resources, including the scientific community, the public, and the NPS conservation and environmental constituencies. Manuscripts are peer-reviewed to ensure that the information is scientifically credible, technically accurate, appropriately written for the intended audience, and is designed and published in a professional manner.

The Natural Resource Technical Reports series is used to disseminate the peer-reviewed results of scientific studies in the physical, biological, and social sciences for both the advancement of science and the achievement of the National Park Service's mission. The reports provide contributors with a forum for displaying comprehensive data that are often deleted from journals because of page limitations. Current examples of such reports include the results of research that addresses natural resource management issues; natural resource inventory and monitoring activities; resource assessment reports; scientific literature reviews; and peer reviewed proceedings of technical workshops, conferences, or symposia.

Views and conclusions in this report are those of the authors and do not necessarily reflect policies of the National Park Service. Mention of trade names or commercial products does not constitute endorsement or recommendation for use by the National Park Service.

Printed copies of reports in these series may be produced in a limited quantity and they are only available as long as the supply lasts. This report is also available from the Heartland I&M Network website (http://www.nature.nps.gov/im/units/HTLN) on the internet, or by sending a request to the address on the back cover.

Please cite this publication as:

NPS D-1249, November 2007

Contents

List of Figures

List of Tables

Appendixes

Abstract

Air quality monitoring for carbon monoxide (CO), particulate matter ($PM_{2.5}$), and meteorological parameters was conducted during the winter of 2006-2007 in Yellowstone National Park at two busy traffic locations. Data from a West Yellowstone monitor and from other seasons at the two in-park monitors were also compared. The CO and $PM_{2.5}$ concentrations are nearly the same as the previous two winter seasons and considerably lower than before the implementation of winter vehicle restrictions. Winter CO concentrations remain higher than the summer CO concentrations when there is much more traffic. $PM_{2.5}$ concentrations are now higher during the summer because of the reduced snowmobile particulate emissions in winter and the frequent incidence of smoke during the summer that is unrelated to vehicle traffic. The restrictions on winter vehicle traffic imposed by the Temporary Winter Use Plan have been effective in bring down air pollution concentrations from values approaching the National Standards to values now less than 25% of the standards. However, winter concentrations are still above the normal background concentrations expected for an isolated continental location where natural conditions should prevale.

Winter Air Quality in Yellowstone National Park
2006 - 2007

Executive Summary

The air quality in Yellowstone National Park was monitored at two locations as part of the adaptive management program on the use of over-snow winter motor vehicles. The leading indicators used were ambient concentrations of carbon monoxide (CO) and particulate matter of 2.5 micrometers or less ($PM_{2.5}$).

The West Entrance near the town of West Yellowstone, MT is the primary indicator for overall air quality and the relationship to traffic, because detailed entry counts could be obtained at that site. A new monitoring station within the town of West Yellowstone shows higher CO and $PM_{2.5}$ concentrations than observed at the park entrance. Old Faithful is a destination for most of the winter use vehicles; CO and $PM_{2.5}$ concentrations are lower at Old Faithful than at the West Entrance.

This report is an update to prior air quality and emission studies. The notable findings this year are:

- Air quality at both the West Entrance and Old Faithful is well below the national ambient air quality standards for human health and considered by EPA to be acceptable. The EPA standard may be too high to be a target concentration for a remote natural area park such as Yellowstone.

- The CO concentrations were about the same as previous years despite an increase in the total number of winter vehicle entries at the west entrance.

- Summer concentrations of CO at the West Entrance and Old Faithful are lower for both the average and peak values than the winter concentrations despite the larger number of vehicles in the summer.

- $PM_{2.5}$ concentrations no longer appear to be correlated to winter traffic at the current traffic volumes. The much lower particulate emissions from snowmobiles with 4-stroke engines have reduced $PM_{2.5}$ concentrations so that other area sources begin to dominate the observed concentrations.

Recommendations

- Winter air quality monitoring should continue to provide feedback on the effectiveness of the Winter Use Plan,

- Restoration of winter air quality to lower concentrations closer to the continental background is recommended for Yellowstone NP. The current mix of winter vehicles are considerably more polluting than light duty passenger vehicles even under the current restrictions.

Acknowledgments

We are grateful for Montana DEQ's assistance and for allowing us to use data back to 1998 when they started West Entrance monitoring station. Gary Nelson and Mary Hektner of the Yellowstone staff were instrumental in setting up the stations and assuring that everything continued to function during the isolation of winter.

Introduction

The effects of winter vehicle exhaust, primarily from snowmobiles, on air quality became an issue in the later 1990's at Yellowstone National Park. For the last several years, ambient air quality monitoring has been conducted at two locations in the Park as part of the adaptive management plan to determine the impact on air quality of implementing the Yellowstone Winter Use Plan.[1]

A guided snowmobile group meets bison on the road, Feb. 2006.
Photo: J. Ray

This report summarizes the carbon monoxide (CO) and particulate matter of 2.5 micrometers or less ($PM_{2.5}$) monitoring data from winter 2006-2007 and gives a historical perspective of monitoring data at the park. The primary interest is trends in air quality that might reflect winter use policy and current conditions compared to the national standards set by the Environmental Protection Agency (EPA).[2]

CO and $PM_{2.5}$ are known health hazards[3] for which EPA has set national standards. In the 1990's the volume of winter vehicle traffic had increased to the point where park staff and visitors were complaining about adverse health effects. Concentrations of CO in the entrance shelters and ambient air along the road were found to be high.[4] Since that time positive-pressure fresh-air ventilation was added to the entrance kiosks and a Best Available Technology (BAT) requirement was set for snowmobiles. The number of snowmobiles entering the park each day has also decreased dramatically. These measures have reduced the CO and $PM_{2.5}$ concentrations at the West Entrance so they no longer are near the national standards[5,6].

Methods

In-park monitoring

Two ambient monitoring locations were used, one at Old Faithful and another at the West Entrance (Figure 1 and Table 1). The Old Faithful shelter was relocated during the summer of 2006 to a site farther east of the old location because of construction on a new visitor center. Instrumentation at the site included a PM$_{2.5}$ monitor (specifically, a Beta Attenuation Monitor), a carbon monoxide (CO) analyzer, wind speed/wind direction sensors, ambient temperature, and a relative humidity sensor. The digital camera also was moved and now shows the parking area next to the temporary visitor center and warming hut (Figures 2, 3, and 4).

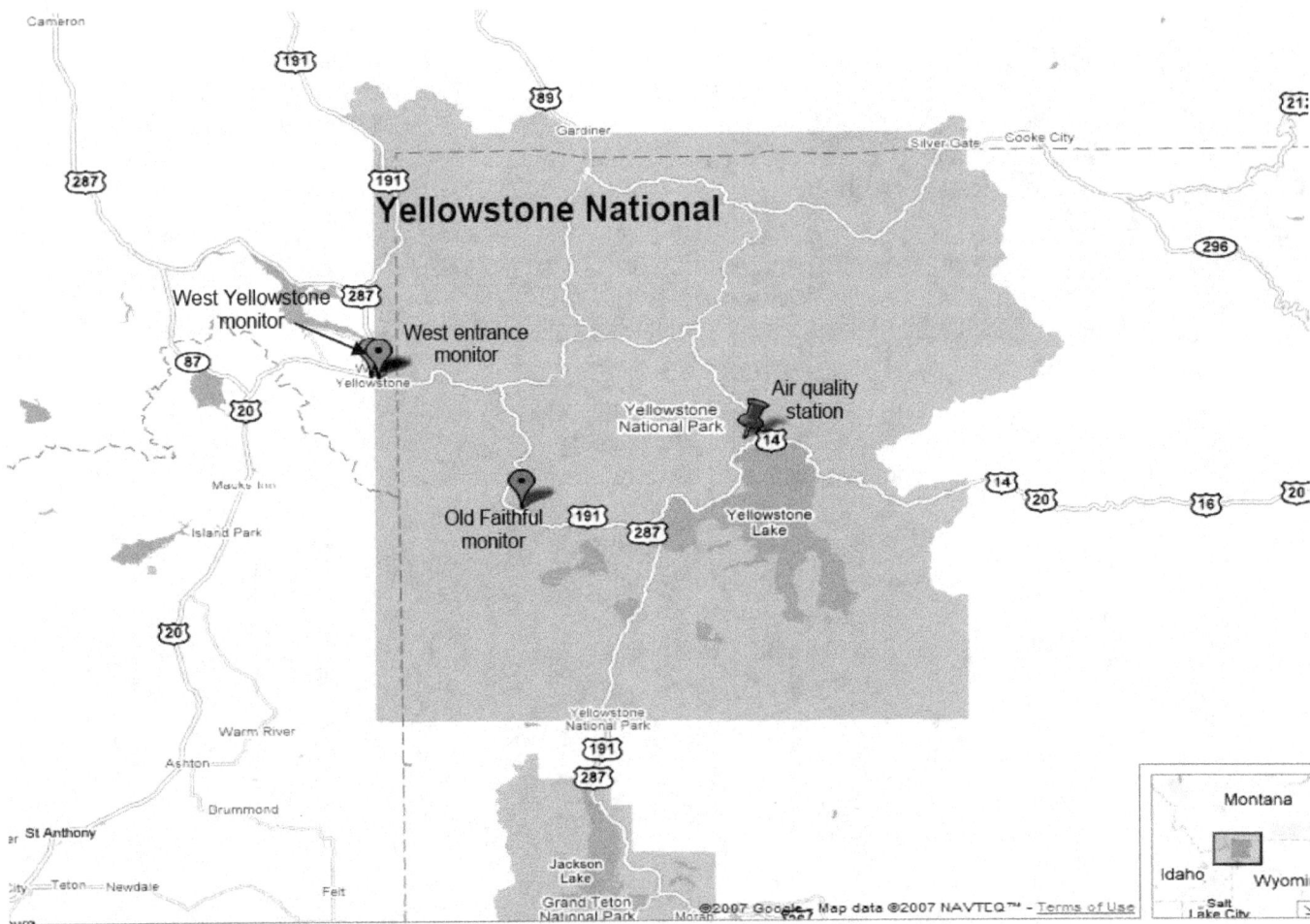

Figure 1. Map with the location of air quality monitors in Yellowstone and nearby during the winter of 2006-2007.

The NPS field support contractor, Air Resource Specialists, in cooperation with park staff, operated the station, processed and validated the data, and provided a data transmittal report. For full details on the monitoring, maps of locations, wind roses, data plots, and data tables, please consult the contractor data reports.[7,8,9]

The State of Montana collected carbon monoxide, PM$_{2.5}$, and meteorological data at the West Entrance of the park in a cooperative effort. Their shelter is located near the out-bound lane on the northeast side of the west entrance canopy (Figure 5).

Data were retrieved from EPA Air Quality System (AQS) database and directly

from the State of Montana, Department of Environmental Quality (DEQ) (http://www.deq.state.mt.us/Air Monitoring/index.asp). All data collection, validation, and quality assurance steps for the West Entrance data were performed by the State of Montana, DEQ.

West Yellowstone Monitoring

The State of Montana opened a new monitoring station in West Yellowstone starting on Jan. 1, 2007. The location is marked on the aerial view in Figure 5 and site information is in Table 1. There are several snowmobile rental businesses and snowcoach departure points with a 3 block radius. This city center monitoring site gives a good identification of the CO and PM$_{2.5}$ concentrations from activities within the resort town.

Figure 2. Monitoring station at Old Faithful in its new location. The winter 2006-2007 location is downwind and northeast of the winter vehicle parking area.

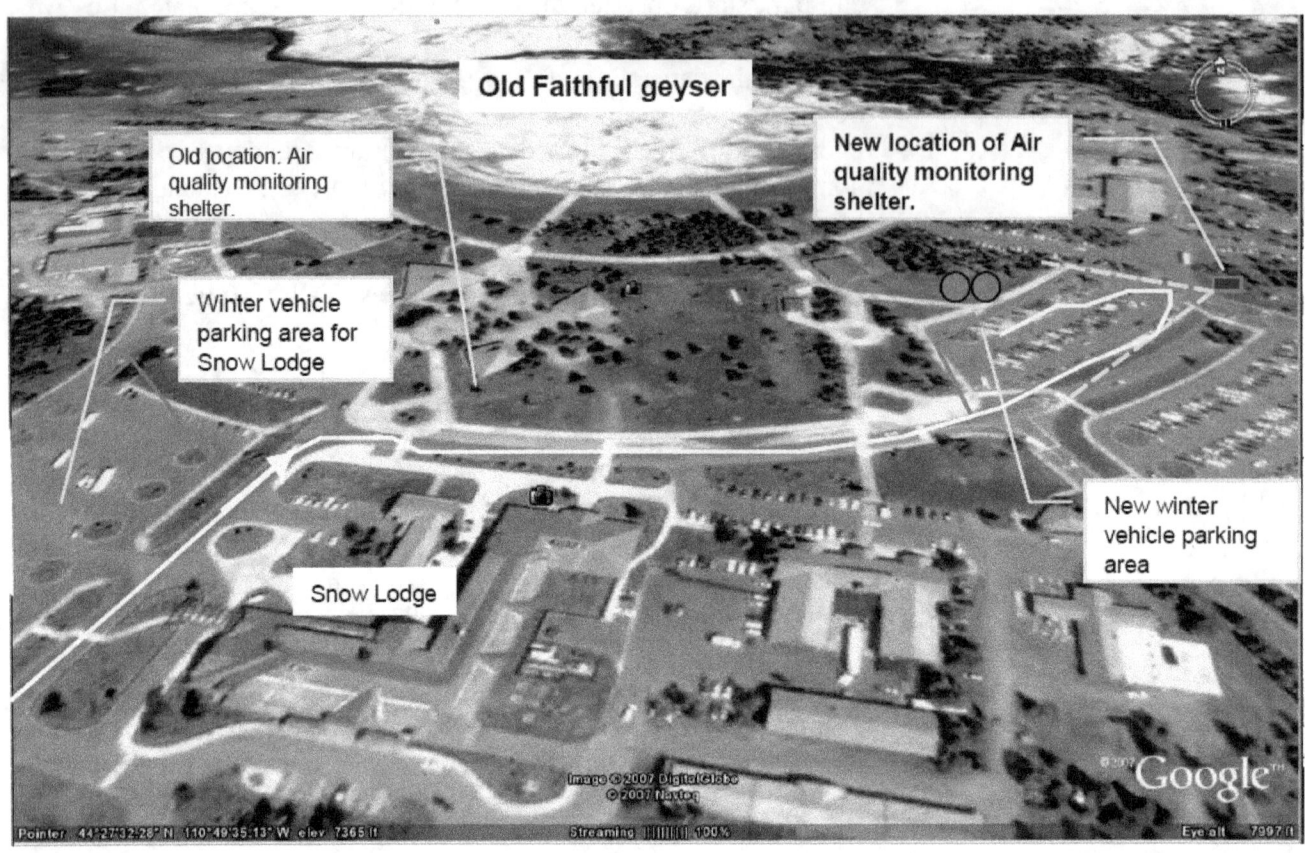

Figure 3. Aerial view of Old Faithful area showing the new locations of the winter vehicle parking and the air quality monitoring station to the east of the old locations. Old Faithful geyser is in the upper background.

Table 1 Monitoring station information for data used in this report.

Site Name	AQS_ID	Latitude	Longitude	Elevation	Parameters
Old Faithful	55-039-1012	44.4569	-110.8314	2246 m	CO, $PM_{2.5}$, winds, temp, solar, RH
West Entrance	30-031-0013	44.6572	-111.0917	2040 m	CO, $PM_{2.5}$, winds, temp,
West Yellowstone	30-031-1001	44.66	-111.10	2041 m	CO, $PM_{2.5}$

Figure 4. Camera view of the parking lot from the new monitoring shelter location at Old Faithful. The cone-shaped roofs of the warning hut and temporary visitor center are seen behind the yellow snowcoaches.

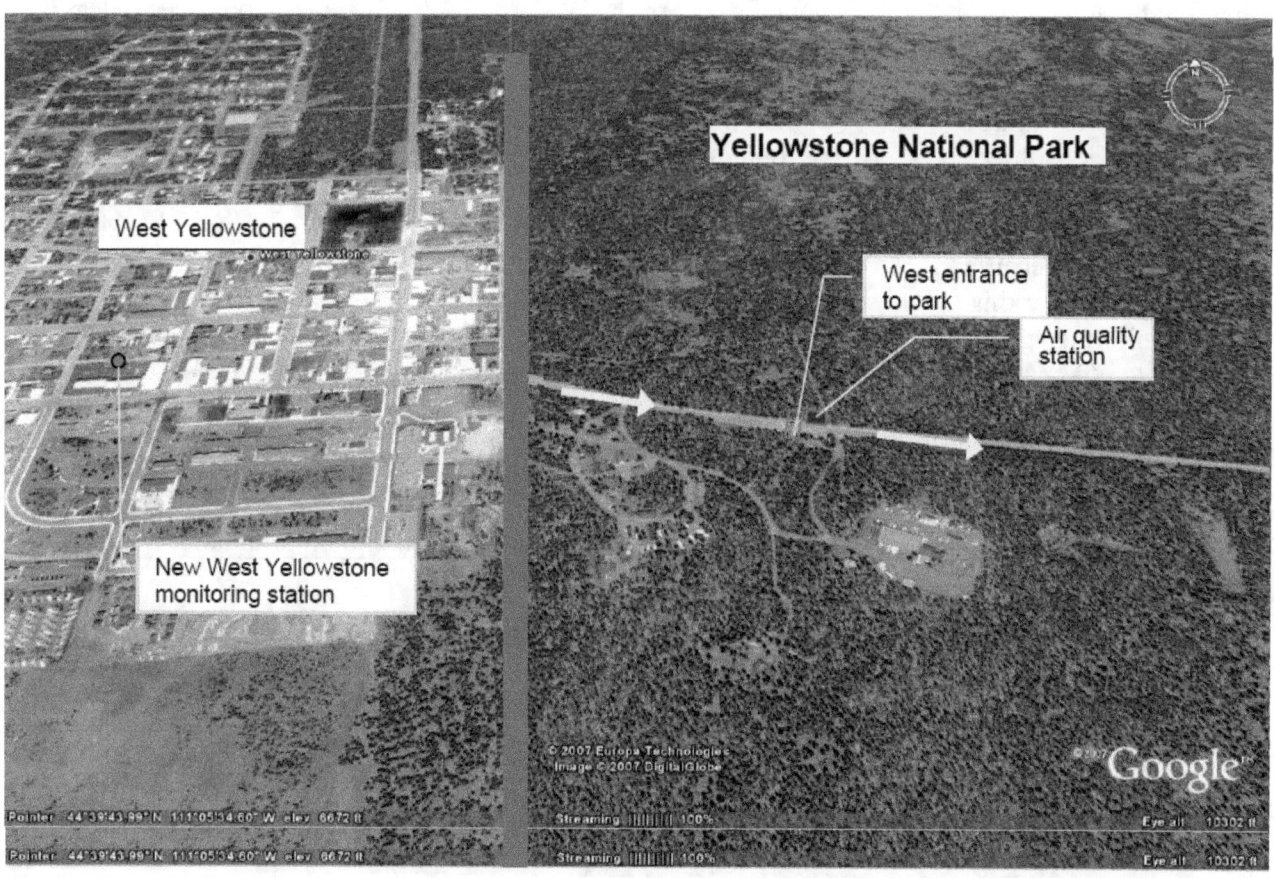

Figure 5. Aerial view of the West Entrance area near the town of West Yellowstone. The air quality monitoring station is on the north side of the road near the roofed entrance structure. Winter vehicles queue up on the west side of the gate. The new monitoring station in West Yellowstone city center is marked with a red dot.

Results and Discussion

Summary statistics

The air quality at both the monitoring stations in Yellowstone National Park remained well below the national standards[2] for carbon monoxide (CO) and particulate matter that was 2.5 micrometers or less in size ($PM_{2.5}$). The winter of 2006-2007 had CO values that were nearly the same as the previous few years. The maximum hourly CO at the West Entrance was slightly higher, but the longer averages of 8-hours and for the season were down. The $PM_{2.5}$ was close to values seen in the previous three years. The CO and $PM_{2.5}$ data at Old Faithful are harder to interpret because the winter vehicle parking and the monitoring station moved due to construction. The lower $PM_{2.5}$ could be because the monitoring station is now farther from conflicting local sources. The CO concentrations are down slightly. This may be due to a different orientation of the monitoring station to the parking area or to a fewer number of vehicles parking near the temporary visitor center.

Tables 2 and 3 have the statistics for comparison to previous years; Table 4 has the relevant values for the standards.[2] For the West Entrance, the maximum 1-hour CO was up from 2.1 ppm in the previous winter to 3.7 ppm in winter of 2006-2007. The maximum 8-hour and the seasonal average CO concentration of 0.8 and 0.2 ppm were down slightly. These values are only a tenth of the CO national standard and represent a significant decrease from 4 years earlier. The daily average and 98th percentile $PM_{2.5}$ concentrations at the West Entrance changed little from the previous couple of years. The timing during the day of $PM_{2.5}$ peaks suggests sources unrelated to the snow vehicle traffic at the entrance[5].

A new monitoring station was installed by the Montana DEQ at a site in West Yellowstone near the city center. Comparison data is provided in Table 5. All the CO and $PM_{2.5}$ concentrations are higher at the city center location than at the park's West Entrance. The daily pattern is somewhat similar to that observed at the West Entrance with a morning peak and a late

Table 2   Statistical comparison of CO (ppm) between Yellowstone NP winter monitoring stations.

	Old Faithful					West Entrance				
Winter CO	2006-2007[1]	2005-2006	2004-2005	2003-2004	2002-2003	2006-2007	2005-2006	2004-2005	2003-2004	2002-2003
Max 1-hr	0.9	1.6	1.6	2.2	2.9	3.7	2.1	2.8	6.4	8.6
% of Std	3%	4%	4%	6%	8%	11%	6%	8%	18%	25%
Max 8-hr	0.4	0.5	0.8	0.9	1.2	0.8	0.9	1.0	1.3	3.3
% of Std	4%	6%	7%	10%	13%	9%	10%	11%	14%	37%
Average	0.27	0.18	0.12	0.26	0.24	0.19	0.23	0.24	0.26	0.57
90th percentile[2]	0.19	0.26	0.29	0.5	0.5	0.27	0.40	0.43	0.5	1.3

1   The visitor parking and the monitoring station moved because of construction at Old Faithful.

2   The 90th percentile is not used by the NAAQS. It is a useful way to track higher concentrations without the points being dominated by possible statistical outliers.

Table 3. Statistical comparison of $PM_{2.5}$ ($\mu g/m^3$) between Yellowstone NP winter monitoring stations.

Winter $PM_{2.5}$	Old Faithful					West Entrance				
	2006-2007[2]	2005-2006	2004-2005	2003-2004	2002-2003	2006-2007	2005-2006	2004-2005	2003-2004	2002-2003
Max 1-hr	20	56	38	151	200	40	44	21	29	81
Max Daily (24-hr)	6.6	9	6	16	37	8.8	7	6	8	15
98th percentile[1]	6.4	9	9	9	21	8.7	6	6	7	17
% of Std	18%	13%	14%	14%	33%	25%	10%	9%	11%	26%
Average	3.3	3.5	4.0	4.9	6.9	2.1	1.9	2.9	4.0	8.2

[1] Statistic that best relates to the NAAQS standard at the time of the measurement (65 $\mu g/m^3$). Based on daily 24-hr average.

2 The visitor parking and the monitoring station moved because of construction at Old Faithful.

Table 4. Ambient Air Quality Standards (AAQS) for carbon monoxide (CO) and particulate matter less than 2.5 micrometers ($PM_{2.5}$).

Standard	Pollutant	1-hr CO (ppm)[1]	8-hr CO (ppm)[1]
National AAQS	CO	35	9
Montana AAQS	CO	23	9
Wyoming AAQS	CO	35	9

Standard	Pollutant	24-hr PM2.5 98th percentile ($\mu g/m^3$)[2]
National AAQS	$PM_{2.5}$	65
New NAAQS[3]	$PM_{2.5}$	35
Montana AAQS	$PM_{2.5}$	65
Wyoming AAQS	$PM_{2.5}$	65

1. Not to be exceeded more than once per year. Link to EPA NAAQS standards http://www.epa.gov/air/criteria.html ; WY DEQ http://deq.state.wy.us/aqd/standards.asp ; MT DEQ http://www.deq.state.mt.us/AirMonitoring/citguide/appendixb.html

2. The 3-year average of the 98th percentile of 24-hour concentrations at each monitor within an area must not exceed 65 $\mu g/m^3$. The winter 98th percentile in the associated tables is given only to demonstrate the improvement between winter seasons. Comparison with the annual standard is not shown. For consistency, the 24-hour day is used to average the hourly $PM_{2.5}$.

3. Revised $PM_{2.5}$ standard by EPA Oct. 2006.

Table 5. Comparison data from the monitoring station in West Yellowstone city center.

Winter CO	Jan-Mar 2006-2007[1]	Units	Winter PM_{25}	Jan-Feb 2006-2007[#]	Units
Max 1-hr	5	ppm	Max 1-hr	119	$\mu g/m^3$
% of National Std (CO)	14%	- -	- -	- -	- -
Max 8-hr	2.4	ppm	Max Daily (24-hr)	32	$\mu g/m^3$
Average	0.48	ppm	Average	10.7	$\mu g/m^3$
90th percentile	0.9	ppm	98th percentile[2]	32	$\mu g/m^3$
% of Std (PM_{25})	- -	- -	% of National Std	91%	- -

1 State operated station in West Yellowstone city center started Jan. 1, 2007. AQS ID = 03-031-0016

2 Statistic that best relates to the NAAQS standard at the time of the measurement (65 $\mu g/m^3$). Based on daily 24-hr average.

afternoon high concentration period that extends into the evening. The city location is expected to have a greater number of winter vehicles and a larger proportion of 2-stroke snowmobiles traveling nearby than any of the park monitoring stations. The higher CO and $PM_{2.5}$ concentrations are consistent with that expectation.

Traffic effects on air quality

The effects of winter traffic in Yellowstone National Park on air quality are best characterized at the West Entrance where both air quality data and detailed traffic counts are available on an hourly basis[10,11]. There is a general trend in the second highest 8-hour CO and the 98th percentile of daily $PM_{2.5}$.

The measured CO and traffic counts at the West Entrance are compared by year. Both the CO and maximum $PM_{2.5}$ concentrations follow the changes in winter traffic and the vehicle emissions (Figure 6 and 7). Over the last three winters the CO concentrations at the West Entrance have been nearly flat. The $PM_{2.5}$ follows a similar pattern at both the West Entrance (Figure 7) and Old Faithful locations.

The daily pattern of air pollutants at the West Entrance follows the times for entrance and exit of the winter vehicles.[11] The peak in the CO concentration is centered on the same 9 am hour as the peak in snowmobile counts. A

secondary CO peak at 5 pm corresponds to the rush of snowmobiles exiting the park. The delay in the $PM_{2.5}$ peak (10 am) and the long tail in the afternoon and evening suggests another PM source besides snowmobiles traveling through the entrance area is contributing.

The entrance counts[10,11] illustrate a difference in when the snowmobiles enter the park compared to the snow coaches. Snowmobiles come in groups led by guides; the period between 8-11 am is when most of the traffic enters. Snow coaches are more spread out during the day, although the West, North, and East gates tend to get most entries during the morning. The snowcoach

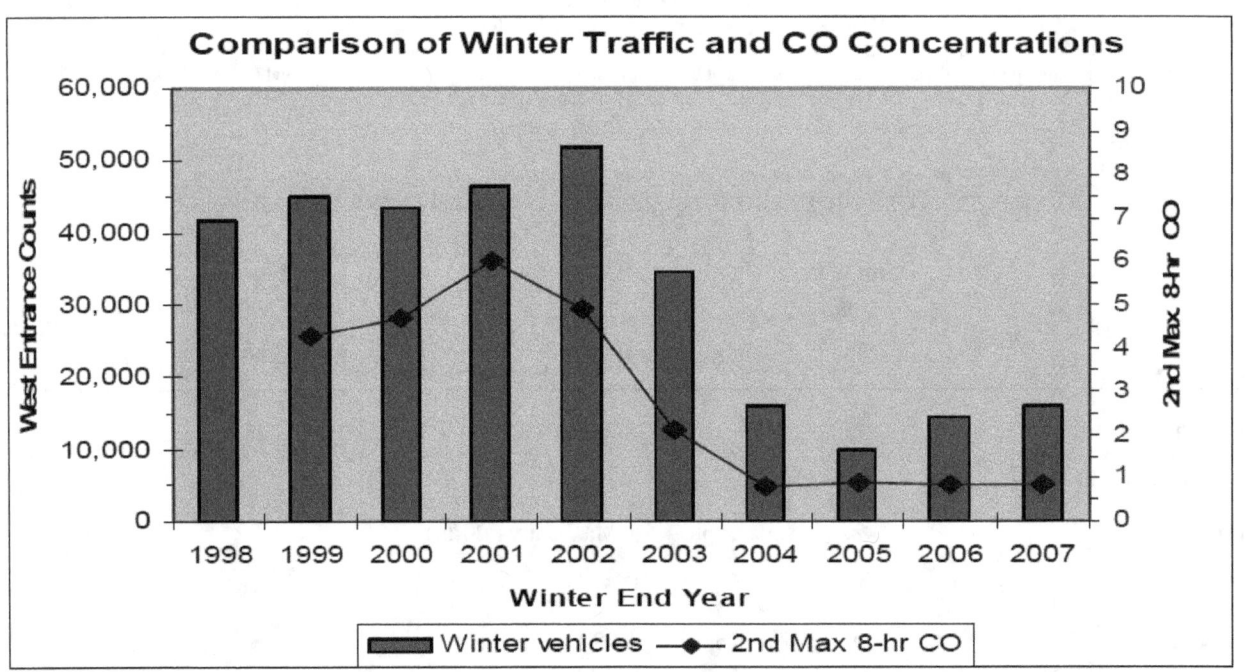

Figure 6. The second highest 8-hour average concentration for the winter season and the amount of traffic through the West Entrance are related. Since 2004 snowmobiles have been all BAT certified.

traffic starts a little earlier and has a second peak midday.

The correspondence between CO and $PM_{2.5}$ to the hourly traffic counts at the West Entrance appears to change daily depending on weather conditions[5]. Figure 8 illustrates how patterns in the observed CO and $PM_{2.5}$ concentrations relate to the traffic counts at the entrance station. The highest peak CO for the day tends to occur in the afternoon and relates to the exiting traffic. There are not hourly vehicle counts for the exiting traffic so the density of vehicles is unknown. Observations and measurements during the remote sensing studies conducted by University of Denver researchers[12] in prior years showed that the average speed was higher for the exiting vehicles.

Peak snowmobile entry is 9-10 am; arrival at Old Faithful is about 2-3 hours later. The CO hourly concentration data has peaks for both entry and exit travel. The exit peak in previous years was smaller, but is now often the larger peak for the day. $PM_{2.5}$ also has a double peak with the afternoon peak much more spread out and even extending until well after dark when there is no traffic exiting the park.

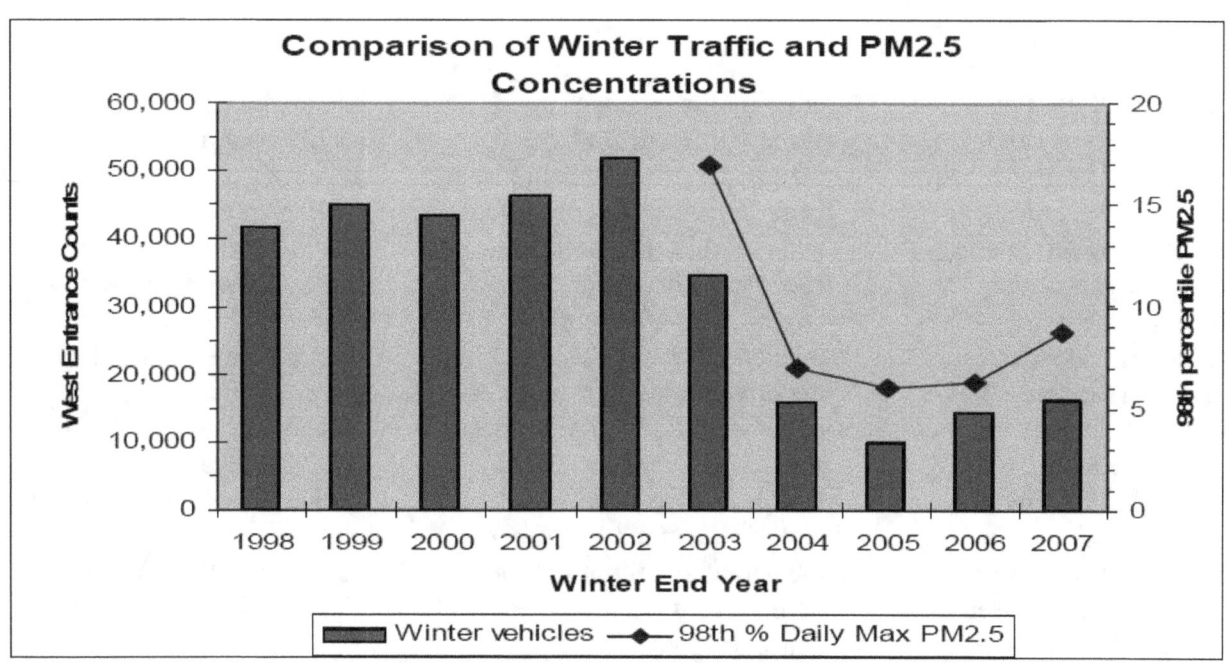

Figure 7. The relationship between the 98th percentile of daily PM2.5 and West Entrance traffic counts are compared here by year.

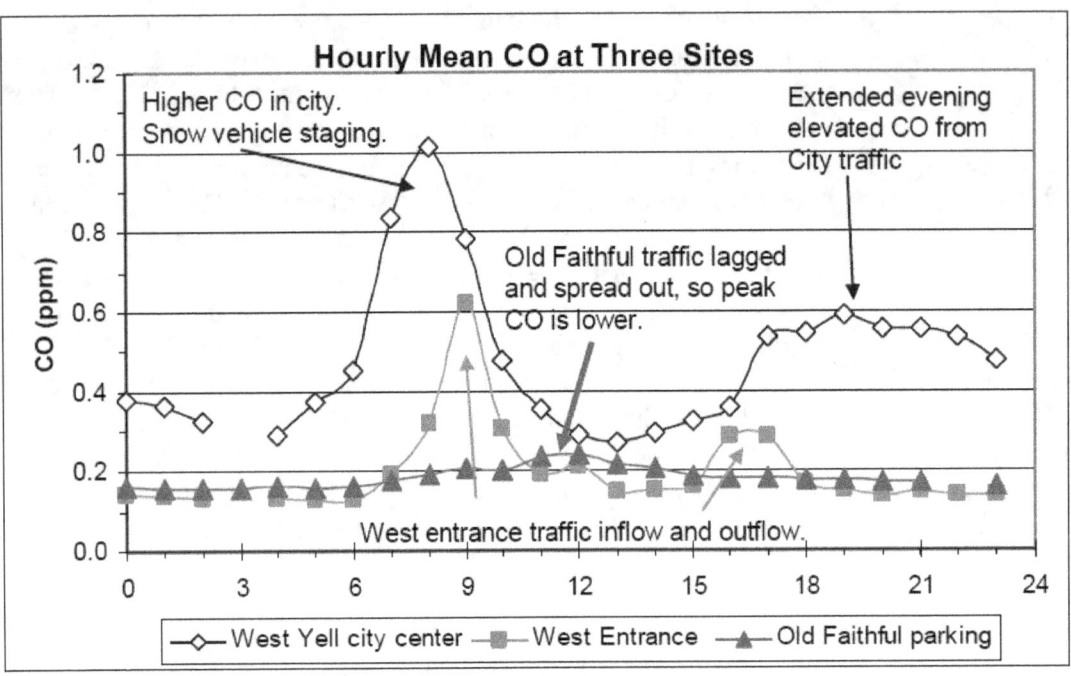

Figure 8. The daily patterns in CO concentration at 3 monitoring location reflect the different traffic patterns in the area. The monitors in the park record less CO than the monitor within the town of West Yellowstone.

The factors that have driven the decreases in CO and $PM_{2.5}$ concentrations over the last several years are fewer snowmobiles entering the park and a switch to cleaner-emitting snowmobiles that meet the BAT (Best Available Technology[1]), mostly by using 4-stroke engines in the snowmobiles. The reduction in aerosol emissions (unburned oil and fuel) from the snowmobiles has been especially noticeable as reduced odor and reduced $PM_{2.5}$.

Winter Traffic Volume

Although the total seasonal number of winter vehicles entering the park was up slightly, it seems to have made little difference on the peak CO and $PM_{2.5}$ observed at the monitoring stations (See Appendix A for the winter 2005-2006 traffic counts). Correlation of CO to the direct number of vehicles counted at the West Entrance was poor. Weather related factors such as wind speed and temperature, that affect the height and timing of the boundary layer, influence the concentrations.

The busiest period for winter vehicles was the period from about Dec. 26, 2006 to Jan. 6, 2007. Figure 9 relates the traffic counts and hourly CO concentrations at the West Entrance. Both a morning and an afternoon peak are seen, as before, but an evening peak also sometimes appears in the record. This is most likely from evening traffic in West Yellowstone. Since there is no traffic through the entrance during the evening hours, the CO and $PM_{2.5}$ observed by the West Entrance monitoring station must come from transport of pollutants from the town of West Yellowstone.

The relationship between traffic volume and peak daily pollutant concentrations is illustrated in Figures 9 and 10 for the busy period between Dec. 26, 2006 and Jan 6, 2007 at the West Entrance.

10

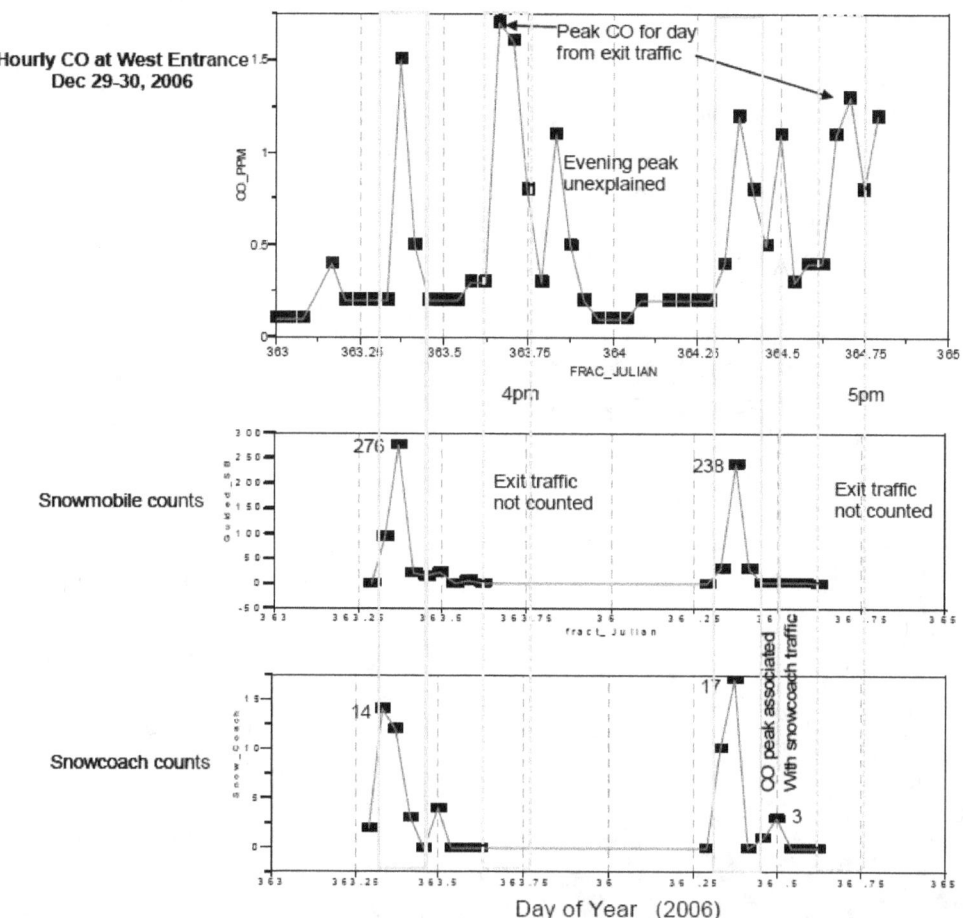

Figure 9. Two busy days (Dec. 29-30, 2006) are used to illustrate relationships between West Entrance traffic counts and observed CO concentrations. The blue boxes and blue-dashed boxes indicate the traffic peaks in morning and afternoon.

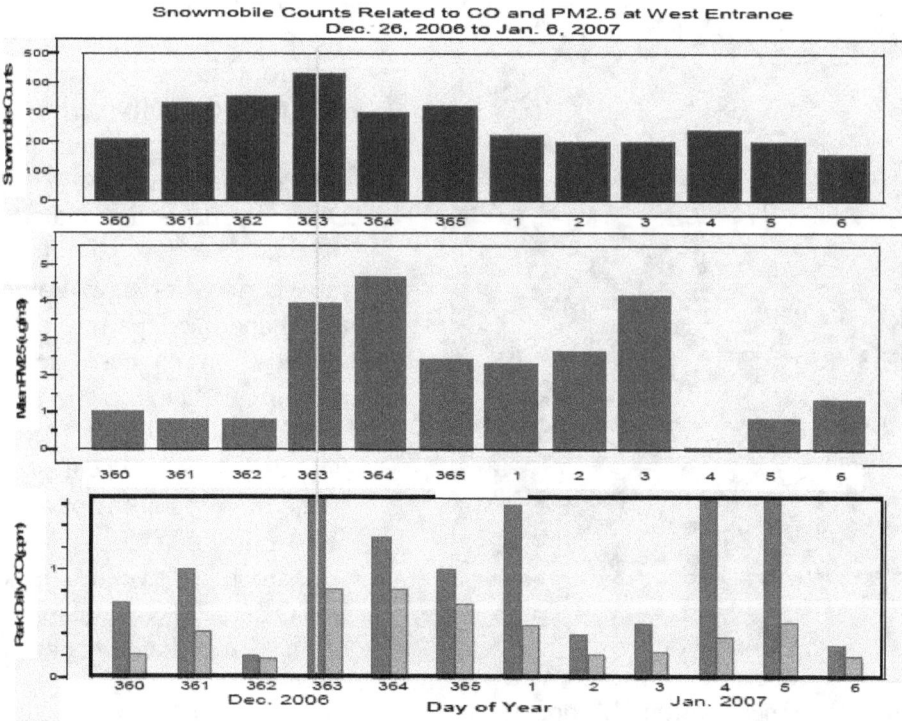

Figure 10. Variations in traffic counts and maximum daily CO and $PM_{2.5}$ concentrations during the busy period between Dec. 26, 2006 and Jan. 6, 2007.

11

Some days ventilate better than others so that a consistent correspondence between and CO concentrations and traffic volume only occurs a few days at a time. Boundary layer conditions and short-term correlations between CO and traffic volume were explored in previous

Dec. 29th when there were 302 snowmobiles and 32 snowcoaches that entered the park at the West Entrance. The exit peak CO was larger than the entrance CO peak (Figure 9). On that same date, the highest CO concentration (0.9 ppm) for the season was observed at Old Faithful (see Figure 11).

It can be noted from Figure 12, where the CO, $PM_{2.5}$ and entrance counts are presented together for the whole winter season at the West Entrance, that peaks only occasional correspond for the three parameters. Obviously, a more complex model to predict peak CO is needed than just a count of snowmobiles.

Data from the West Yellowstone city center monitor (Figure 13) illustrates the daily variations in the broader town area as a source of CO and $PM_{2.5}$. Diurnal patterns are related to the visitor activity and the busy periods for snowmobile rental and the departure of loaded snowcoaches. The morning CO peak at the city center is slightly earlier and larger than the CO peak seen in the morning at the park's West Entrance station. Afternoon and evening peaks in CO and $PM_{2.5}$ are also often seen at the city center site.

Image of an old poster found in West Yellowstone showing the

heritage of the snowmobile back to the snow coach invented by Armand Bombardier.

reports.[5,6] The highest CO concentration (1.7 ppm) during the period occurred on

Old Faithful

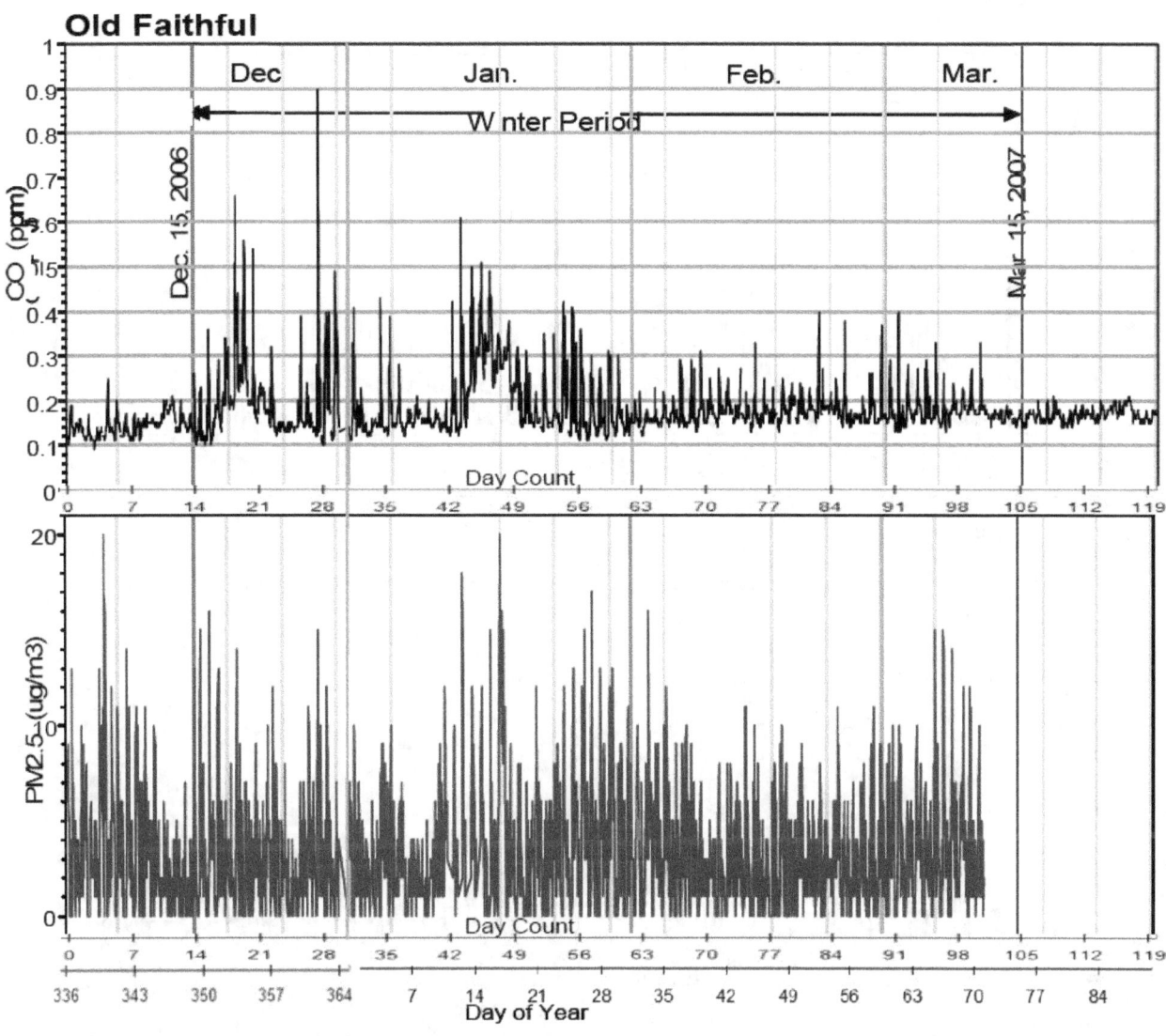

Figure 11.   Hourly concentration data for CO and PM2.5 at Old Faithful from Dec. 1, 2006 to Mar. 31, 2007. Note the lower scales than in Figure 12.

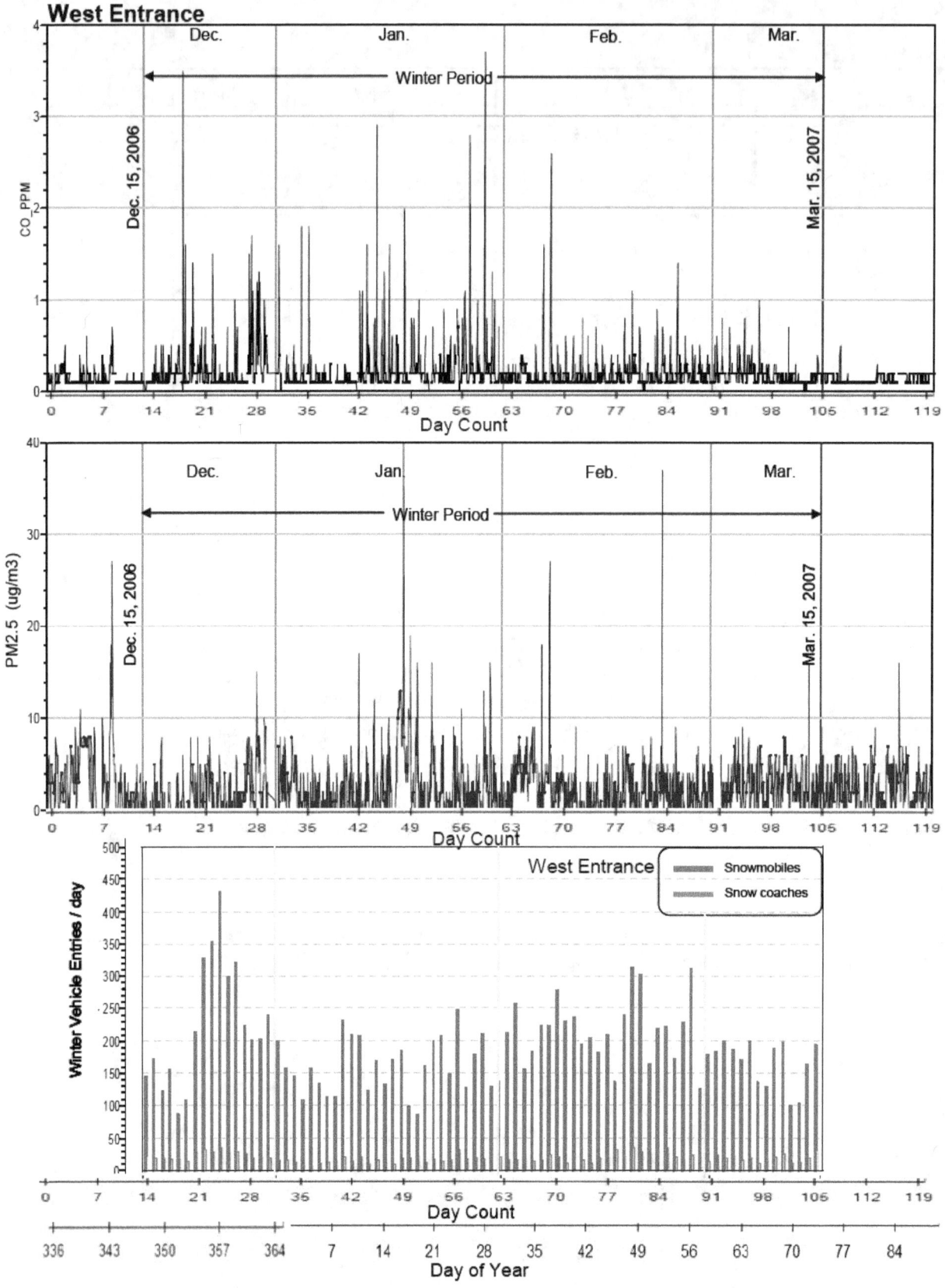

Figure 12. Hourly concentration data for CO and PM$_{2.5}$ at the West Entrance from Dec. 1, 2006 to Mar. 31, 2007. Bottom bar chart has the number of winter vehicles entering the West Entrance each day.

14

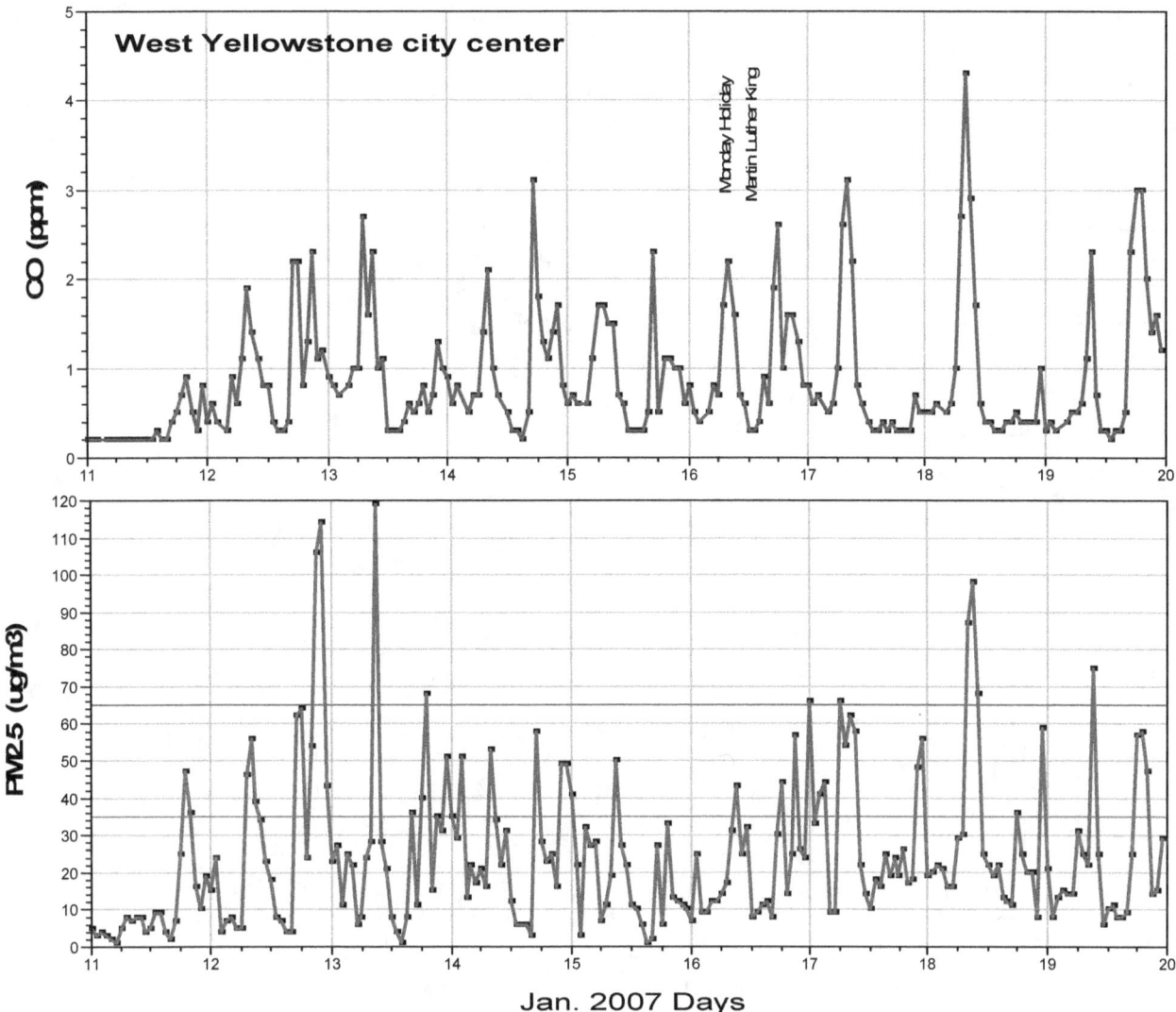

Figure 13. CO and PM$_{2.5}$ hourly concentrations from the West Yellowstone city center monitoring station. Note the expanded scales. The period from Jan. 11, to Jan. 19, 2007 includes the busy Martin Luther King holiday (Jan. 16).

Seasonal Air Quality

The seasonal variation in CO concentrations shows the influence of different traffic volumes and types. The background concentrations[5,13] for Yellowstone have been estimated at 0.1 – 0.2 ppm; remote locations have background concentrations in the 0.05 to 0.10 ppm range, In Figure 14 the mean CO concentrations are plotted by season over 2 years. The mean CO concentrations at both locations are elevated over the background. The summer CO concentrations are lower than the winter concentrations while the Spring and Fall periods, when the park roads are closed to visitor traffic, are basically at background levels. Greater detail can be obtained from Table 6.

The maximum seasonal CO concentrations are also highest in winter and lower in summer, despite the large difference in the volume of vehicles between seasons. During Spring and Fall there are some periods of slightly higher CO, such that the maximum hourly values are above the background.

The 3 winter periods (Figure 14) have roughly the same

CO concentrations. BAT snowmobiles and 4-stroke engines were used in all 3 of these years. Old Faithful generally had slightly lower CO concentrations than the West Entrance where traffic tended to be denser.

Summer PM$_{2.5}$ concentrations can be much higher than the values observed in the winter. Smoke and other particulates account for most of the summertime PM.

Table 6 shows that summer and fall of 2006 were especially bad. The smoke in summer of 2006 was from the western region, not from wildfires in the park. PM$_{2.5}$ concentrations fall off in the Spring right after the roads are closed to winter vehicle traffic and before the fire season begins.

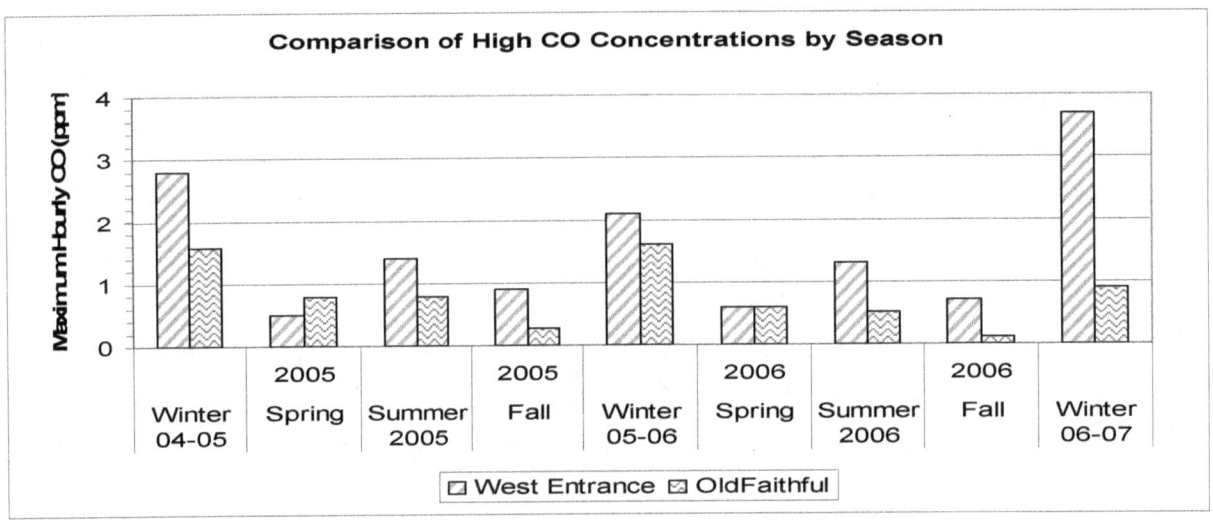

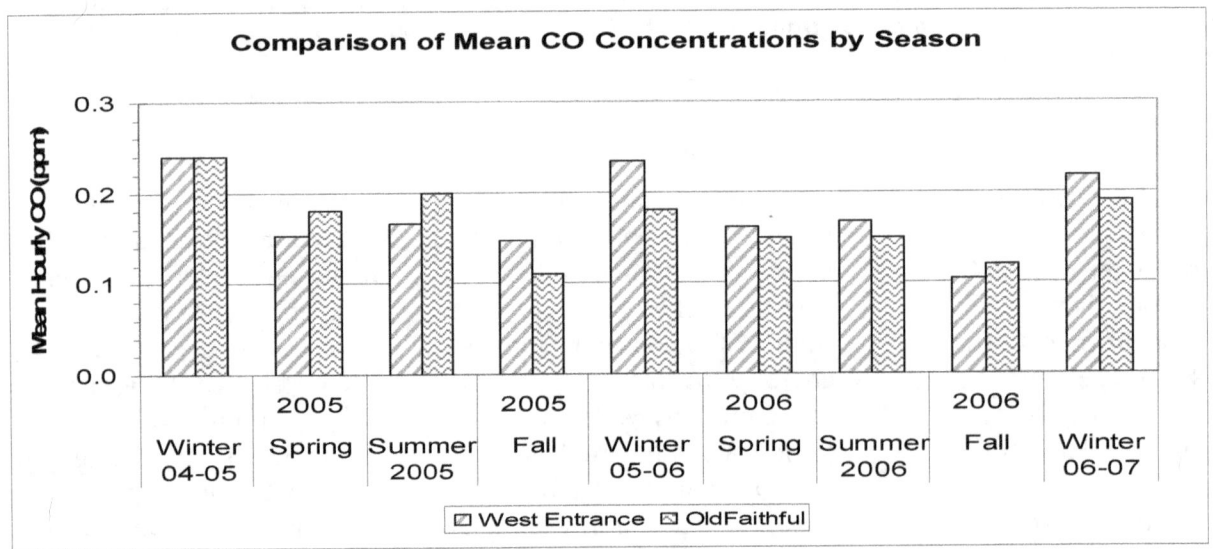

Figure 14. Comparison of maximum and mean CO concentrations in different seasons for West Entrance and Old Faithful. Summer concentrations are lower than winter even though there is much more traffic in the summer.

16

Table 6. Seasonal statistical summary for CO and PM$_{2.5}$ at the West Entrance[1].

	West Entrance								
Statistics for CO ⬇	**Winter 04-05**	**Spring 2005**	**Summer 2005**	**Fall 2005**	**Winter 05-06**	**Spring 2006**	**Summer 2006**	**Fall 2006**	**Winter 06-07**
Max. 1-hr	2.80	0.50	1.40	0.90	2.10	0.60	1.30	0.70	3.70
Max. 8-hr	0.96	0.26	0.61	0.35	0.91	0.33	0.86	0.41	0.83
Season average	0.24	0.15	0.17	0.15	0.23	0.16	0.17	0.10	0.22
90th percentile	0.40	0.20	0.30	0.20	0.40	0.20	0.30	0.20	0.40
Statistics for PM$_{2.5}$ ⬇	**Winter 04-05**	**Spring 2005**	**Summer 2005**	**Fall 2005**	**Winter 05-06**	**Spring 2006**	**Summer 2006**	**Fall 2006**	**Winter 06-07**
Max. 1-hr	21	16	84	21	44	15	111	262	40
Max. 24-hr	6.0	6.0	14.0	6.5	13.3	4.1	55.3	37.1	8.8
Season average	3.0	2.6	3.9	1.7	2.1	1.8	6.3	3.6	2.0
98th percentile	6.0	6.0	11.3	6.5	10.2	4.1	30.8	37.1	5.7
Period	Dec 15 – Mar 15	Mar 16 – Apr 19	Apr 20 – Oct 31	Nov 1 – Nov 30	Dec 15 – Mar 15	Mar 16 – Apr 19	Apr 20 – Oct 31	Nov 1 – Nov 30	Dec 15 – Mar 15

1   CO as ppm; PM2.5 as $\mu g/m^3$

Conclusion

Direct measurements at two locations within Yellowstone National Park, the West Entrance and Old Faithful, show that air quality has improved during the last several years. The magnitude of peak CO events and the overall concentration and number of events are below the standards set by EPA to protect human health. Peak 1-hour and 8-hour CO concentrations in the winter are elevated over the background concentration and are higher than in the summer when traffic volume is much greater.

Small changes in either daily or seasonal traffic counts have not made large differences in the CO concentrations at either the West Entrance or Old Faithful.

Seasonal average CO concentrations for winter are higher than summer, but within a factor of two. By contrast, the summer $PM_{2.5}$ concentrations are higher than the winter peak and average values. The summer $PM_{2.5}$ peak values are unrelated to Yellowstone traffic; a summer relationship to wildfire smoke was shown in a previous report[5]. There were two days in summer of 2006 when $PM_{2.5}$ exceeded the 35 $\mu g/m^3$ limit of the national standard, but no winter days have had exceedances.

The BAT controls on snowmobiles and limits on the number of snowmobiles, as applied by the Temporary Winter Use Plan, have helped reduce the CO and $PM_{2.5}$ concentrations in the park. Monitoring of winter air quality will continue as part of the Adaptive Management Plan as the permanent Winter Use Plan gets implemented.

Winter vehicle traffic along the road to Old Faithful.
Photo: J. Ray

Literature Cited

1. Yellowstone Temporary Winter Use Plan and other Winter Use Technical Documents
   http://www.nps.gov/yell/parkmgmt/winterusetechnicaldocuments.htm

2. EPA, National Ambient Air Quality Standards (NAAQS)   http://www.epa.gov/ttn/naaqs/

3. EPA, CO and PM effects on health   http://www.epa.gov/air/urbanair/6poll.html

4. National Park Service, Air Quality Division, Feb., 2000. *Quality Concerns Related to Snowmobile Usage in National Parks*. Available from:
   http://www2.nature.nps.gov/air/studies/yell/20042005yellWinterSummary.cfm

5. Ray, J. D., 2006. Winter Air Quality in Yellowstone National Park: 2005 – 2006, Air Resources Technical Report NPS/ARD/2007/D-1207. National Park Service, Denver, Colorado. Available from: http://www2.nature.nps.gov/air/Pubs/index.cfm

6. Ray, J. D., 2005. *2004-2005 Yellowstone Winter Air Quality Overview Report*, NPS Air Resources Division, Denver, CO. Available from:
   http://www2.nature.nps.gov/air/Pubs/index.cfm

7. *Data Transmittal Report for the Yellowstone National Park Winter Use Air Quality Study, 2004-2005* – Mar. 15, 2006, Air Resource Specialists, Ft Collins, CO (August, 2006). Available from: http://www2.nature.nps.gov/air/Pubs/index.cfm

8. *Data Transmittal Report for the Yellowstone National Park Winter Use Air Quality Study, 2005-2006* –Aug, 2006, Air Resource Specialists, Ft Collins, CO (August, 2006). Available from: http://www2.nature.nps.gov/air/Pubs/index.cfm .

9. *Data Transmittal Report for the Yellowstone National Park Winter Use Air Quality Study, 2006-2007* – July 2007, Air Resource Specialists, Ft Collins, CO (July 2007). Available from: http://www2.nature.nps.gov/air/Pubs/index.cfm .

10. National Park Service, Public Use Statistics, Yellowstone visitor and vehicle count statistics
    http://www2.nature.nps.gov/mpur/

11. Troy Davis, 2007. Personal communication, Hourly records of vehicle entries collected by ranger staff.

12. Bishop, Gary A., R. Stadtmuller, D. H. Stedman, and John D. Ray, 2007. *Portable Emission Measurements of Snowcoaches and Snowmobiles in Yellowstone National Park*, University of Denver, Dept. of Chemistry and Biochemistry, Denver, CO. Available from:
    www.feat.biochem.du.edu

13. P. Warneck, 1988. *Chemistry of the Natural Atmosphere*, Academic Press, New York, pp.158-159.

Appendix A   West Entrance Traffic Counts

Daily winter vehicle counts from the Yellowstone NP West Entrance.[8] The average daily snowmobile count was 169, maximum daily count was 340.

Date	Snowmobiles	Snowcoaches		Date	Snowmobiles	Snowcoaches
20-Dec-2006	136	21		31-Jan-2007	121	14
21-Dec-2006	170	19		1-Feb-2007	124	19
22-Dec-2006	120	21		2-Feb-2007	206	16
23-Dec-2006	149	15		3-Feb-2007	247	16
24-Dec-2006	89	19		4-Feb-2007	146	13
25-Dec-2006	106	14		5-Feb-2007	170	9
26-Dec-2006	207	28		6-Feb-2007	214	12
27-Dec-2006	318	32		7-Feb-2007	211	20
28-Dec-2006	340	31		9-Feb-2007	212	12
29-Dec-2006	302	32		10-Feb-2007	234	22
30-Dec-2006	289	31		11-Feb-2007	182	16
31-Dec-2006	320	26		12-Feb-2007	194	9
1-Jan-2007	215	28		13-Feb-2007	175	17
2-Jan-2007	199	19		14-Feb-2007	195	18
3-Jan-2007	195	18		15-Feb-2007	121	28
4-Jan-2007	222	20		16-Feb-2007	224	20
5-Jan-2007	192	14		17-Feb-2007	299	28
6-Jan-2007	147	13		18-Feb-2007	294	25
7-Jan-2007	138	11		19-Feb-2007	154	20
8-Jan-2007	100	8		20-Feb-2007	209	14
9-Jan-2007	155	8		21-Feb-2007	197	29
10-Jan-2007	123	11		22-Feb-2007	162	21
11-Jan-2007	108	13		23-Feb-2007	220	18
12-Jan-2007	83	14		24-Feb-2007	299	22
13-Jan-2007	214	23		25-Feb-2007	119	17
14-Jan-2007	202	14		26-Feb-2007	161	12
15-Jan-2007	194	16		27-Feb-2007	168	17
16-Jan-2007	100	9		28-Feb-2007	183	20
17-Jan-2007	156	16		1-Mar-2007	173	18
18-Jan-2007	127	11		2-Mar-2007	162	16
19-Jan-2007	166	10		3-Mar-2007	189	17
20-Jan-2007	181	21		4-Mar-2007	131	10
21-Jan-2007	91	17		5-Mar-2007	123	16
22-Jan-2007	76	19		6-Mar-2007	178	17
23-Jan-2007	145	9		7-Mar-2007	184	23
24-Jan-2007	188	15		8-Mar-2007	91	11
25-Jan-2007	194	15		9-Mar-2007	94	12
26-Jan-2007	137	13		10-Mar-2007	156	18
27-Jan-2007	230	26		11-Mar-2007	185	24
28-Jan-2007	120	14		8-Feb-2007	263	20
29-Jan-2007	171	14				
30-Jan-2007	197	19		**Winter Totals**	**14,682**	**1,453**

Appendix B   Data Access

Air monitoring and emission study reports, journal publications, and data:
http://www2.nature.nps.gov/air/studies/yell/20042005yellAQwinter.cfm

Hourly CO, PM2.5, and meteorological data:
http://12.45.109.6/

MT DEQ's West Entrance monitoring station data and station information:
http://www.deq.state.mt.us/AirMonitoring/index.asp

Other MT DEQ monitoring stations:
http://www.deq.state.mt.us/AirMonitoring/sites/QueryAQsitelocation.asp

Old Faithful area webcam, current weather, and current pollutant data:
(http://www2.nature.nps.gov/air/WebCams/parks/yellcam/yellcam.htm

NPS D-1249, November 2007